THE NATIONAL POETRY SERIES

The National Poetry Series was established in 1978 to ensure the publication of five poetry books annually through participating publishers. Publication is funded by the late James A. Michener, the Copernicus Society of America, Edward J. Piszek, the Lannan Foundation, the National Endowment for the Arts, and the Tiny Tiger Foundation.

2002 COMPETITION WINNERS

Meredith Stricker of Carmel, California, *Tenderness Shore*
Chosen by Fred Chappell, published by Louisiana State University Press

Julie Kane of Natchitoches, Louisiana, *Rhythm & Booze*
Chosen by Maxine Kumin, published by University of Illinois Press

William Keckler of Harrisburg, Pennsylvania, *Sanskrit of the Body*
Chosen by Mary Oliver, published by Viking Penguin

Eleni Sikelianos of Boulder, Colorado, *Footnotes to the Lambs*
Chosen by Diane Ward, published by Green Integer

Gabriel Spera of Los Angeles, California, *The Standing Wave*
Chosen by Dave Smith, published by HarperCollins

tenderness shore

Meredith Stricker

LOUISIANA STATE UNIVERSITY PRESS · BATON ROUGE
2003

12   11   10   09   08   07   06   05   04   03
5   4   3   2   1

DESIGNER: Andrew Shurtz
TYPEFACE: Minion
PRINTER AND BINDER: Thomson-Shore, Inc.

Library of Congress Cataloging-in-Publication Data:

Stricker, Meredith.
    Tenderness shore / Meredith Stricker.
        p. cm. — (The national poetry series)
    ISBN 0-8071-2876-7 (alk. paper)
        I. Title. II. Series.

    PS3619.T747T46 2003
    811'.6—dc21

                    2002043416

The author gratefully acknowledges the editors of the following journals, in which some of the poems in this collection appeared previously, sometimes in slightly altered form: *Conjunctions:* "Lexicon of the Muse"; *The Pedestal Magazine* (an on-line journal): "reading the blank spaces"; *Ploughshares:* "Threshing the Word: Sappho and a Particle Physics of Language." The greater part of "Sappho's Sparrows" appeared on *Conjunctions'* web site, including "Sappho, though the technology has changed," "inhabited by your absence," "a telegram from S," "maps to the cliff edge," "the quality of mercy," "the orchard," "dear reader," "shopping list," "to speak in smells as one animal to another," "'blue: the sea, the sky the unknown,'" and "lumen: light, eye, opening."

Portrait of Albert Camus (p. 56), écrivain français, Paris, © 1944 Henri Cartier-Bresson/Magnum Photos. Image of Höllentalklamm (p. 66), postcard from the author's collection, Aufnahmne and Verlag Paul Seichte, Foto-Centrale, Obergrainau.

μουσομανεο: *to be Muse mad, smitten by the Muses*

dedication: for the Muses and Sappho, the tenth along with all those others who have shone here — your images, exchanges, teachings are abundant and unfathomable as ever. I open these pages to you: for T, without end and also E: Eva, Eurydice, Elizabeth, for FLS, patron saint of books and children, S and A, cartographers of the unknown, the sisters McV, and YSM, MY (her China and witness), HJ and animal tracks, scattered *room-mates*, also L (across breaches) and DM (bridge to HD and Cage), Frances and Walker, KF and *HOW(ever),* DB, K and W, S and J for their world of color, T and K, Cixous, the sparks off Zoe's fur, all the light in new green grasses, GS (Blake's wayward cousin and conspirator), SW and SW (for seeing and seeing into), Cecilia Vicuña's threads and weave, J (the future), N Freedom, Nathalie Babel Brown and her 19th century, V Woolf, Schwitters, Elytis, Beuys, O'Keefe, Rexroth, Chaiken, Rainier, Twombly, Snyder, Berger, numberless sentient beings: fireflies, smooth granite rocks, lemon trees, moving water, lilacs in the alley, white paper, olive trees, live oaks, all bees, groves: their immense silence and open-hearted light

CONTENTS

intense
kalloni
karaghiosis
literature
luna
midday
mithymna
musica
nai
night
odysseus
ψ
$\odot$
$\therefore$
$\Pi\varepsilon\tau\rho\alpha$
quiet
roses
shepherds
squid
taverna
traffic
undergrowth
villa
widow
winnowing ring
white line
words
X

sappho's sparrows

A SERIES OF MESSAGES, EXCHANGES & ENCOUNTERS

"beautiful swift sparrows whirring fast-beating wings . . .
above the dark earth . . . through the mid-air"
— Sappho, fragment 1

"Some say there are nine Muses. How careless!
Look, Sappho of Lesbos is the tenth."
— Plato, *Palatine Anthology*

Sappho, though the technology has changed

I am walking straight toward you, listening.

Dry grass and American words are all I have

to reach you. And this small clay figure of a boy

whose belly is warm with dust, the thumbprint

warm on the boy who makes us lie down

and we lie down so that even flies love

our skin and a woman speaks dark in each ear.

While in this bright air, a man is hammering

against marble that flares everything white

in the sound of cicadas and wind. The invisible

is not hiding. Appearance is not hollow

clothing. Not a shell. The doves are your doves.

Not emblems. Not hidden. They are close as

the water's clear salt and where my heart dives no less.

inhabited by your absence

> *only one complete poem survives from Sappho's nine books of lyrics*

plowed field just at sunset

stones, black sea urchins, sand
the wash of salt

candles, soap, white cup from the trellised marketplace
bells, counting aloud

everywhere your words have been torn away

scant shelter of thistles, thin rain, shadow puppets, the moon
yellow over blue Asia Minor

each fragment — a lacuna of perception — shadows the unseen

clear glass of water
the sound of waves

just as transparent as olive groves
drawing light into their leaves and fruit

there are so many places to find you

in the endless

white spaces you have left us

■

a telegram from S
hastily translated

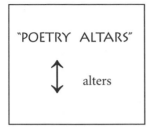

BELIEVE THIS

LUCENT MOUTH FLOWERING

SHRINES: EVERYTHING SEEN

(no exclusion)

later, a footnote appeared on green paper
wrapped around a stone near the porch steps

EROS - TRANSFORMATIONAL ACTIVITY - THE POEM

A LONG FALL INTO
INTELLIGENCE

in love with

WHITE CLIFF EDGE,
PATH THROUGH CYPRESS, WHERE WE'RE HEADED

eyes open

maps to the cliff edge

. . . . what is visible . . . .

. . . .

carries us inside . . . .

. . . . [what is visible] . . . . takes us close

. . . . as the moon . . . .   /

increases . . . . what is visible increases

. . . . recovers . . . . [is shining]

. . . . and clear, cicadas . . . . the actual

grows larger . . . . takes us far . . . .

[is not hiding] . . . .

. . . . Ochre wax . . . .

. . . . [white] . . . .

. . . . washed rock . . . .

oregano . . . . a gate . . . . [Young mother]

. . . . blue swallow . . . . It is not a trick . . . .

. . . . this gravel path . . . .

laurel leaves . . . .

. . . . climbing roses

. . . .

. . . .

we are . . . .

 . . . . not

turned away . . .

. . . .

the quality of mercy

holds out her hand . . . . . . I go walking in the dark
. . . . porcelain face in the grass . . . .
worn, milky blue, a charm . . . .
. . . . Her face is sepia and gentle . . . .
. . . . come to me beyond all roses and praise
. . . .
My heart is a grammar lesson lark

who sings as the grain beats green on our legs, a field

that flame does not burn, it must be light, it must be secret

our walking there . . . . . . hollows in the turf . . . .
. . . . white stones in a line . . . .
the machines can't mow water down . . . .

she raises the light in her hand
. . . .

. . . . across the night field

all that is lost . . . .

the orchard

"as the sweet-apple reddens on the bough-top"
— Sappho, fragment 105

mutsu, keepsake, russet:
irregular, fertile treasury
of names in the mouth

eating the imagined

we lie in late
fall grasses deep
green moving inside

caves of happiness

the creek shines nearby
for coyotes, foxes and deer
invisible in this wild

garden, temporary
peace between the cultivated

and what lives outside our naming

stealing persimmons

how good the clear cold air —

stars, our long branch

tenderness shore

*"Down from the blue sky
Came Eros taking off his clothes
His shirt of Phoenician red."*
— Sappho, fragment 54

It isn't this spring alone you'll find me

adrift on brocade cushions

the salt now dry on his body

hair smelling of smoke and leaves

I like the unspoken

tangled with breath

He is expecting a common with supplies first.

the more we surrender

Sounds come close to us as deer

bees drown in blossom heavy oleander

as a spring crosses the courtyard

and it is suddenly clear

the land drawn on maps is real.

Entire fields of sunflowers between Istanbul

and the coast. White steps down to water.

Bees there on a pitcher, and yes, it is wet.

shopping list

purple & russet silk

gold flame pattern

birdwing throat

scent of sunflower pollen

myrrh & pale jasmine

iridescent water cloth

grass green rose dust

falls loosely over shoulders

plum leaf: haze, light

spilling water bowl, a morning

of skin skimming freshly woven

tracking sappho

in the spirit of maps that tell you everything
except how to get there:

⋰•• ruins, bees, pollen
green at the interior

 olive groves, laurels

∩ thermal waters, salamanders,
aquamarine

 coves, sheltered bays,
fishnetting

▽ temple, relics, subway graffiti
owl

 writing, messages, signs

◖ moon, silver, water
silence

□ pomegranate, sun, black
clay shards, bowls

 sanctuaries, shelter
altars, canyons

 mother of pearl, scent
fine cloths

 springs, oleander, saplings
in sidewalks

 roadway, neural net,
intuition, correspondences

• memory, mercy

 signature, absence

questionnaire

"*I talked with you in a dream, Kypris-born Aphrodite*"
— Sappho, fragment 134

Dear S,

source code Have you ever had the kind of dream that leaves you

more tired, more undergrounded upon awakening?

carrying you like a hollow bark in a flooded creek?

Dreams that are thick as wool,   incessant as fever?

site Where do dreams come from — our mind

or the world outside scented with clover?

Is it possible to tell the difference?

afterlife Is it hard to leave the body

becoming cloud,   fractal edged leaf?

If all is given away,

does anything return?   Are dreams where the gods

die into their immortality   shiny as flint

evanescent as steam so language remains
perishing
the only attribute of the body to stay alive?
endlessly
Whose is the light flaring this corolla?

14

dear reader

clever, brutal, cold:
no one ever accused me of that

unsolicited advice: think of television as something you watch

rather than it watching you
wearing you like a string of loose beads

secret of my universe?

— bursting, ripe in my own skin
— delighting in thunder (περπικεραυνοσ)
— like a flower bud

— three senses of the word ακη:
    1. a point edge   2. silence   3. healing

You wanted a picture of me

ok, here it is:

[farther along the stream: a wild pear
ΚΟΠΠΟΣ: the hollow between two waves]

yours,

Σ

as stars move in rhythm

constellate   sycamore leafed, pollen edged patterns

their light is time

"One Greek word combines dance and song, the word *Molpe*.
Metron means measurement and the things measured are the *feet* or *steps* on which
the words of the song move. For the words had to dance with the dancers."

"...TO GO THERE...THIS...MIND...MUCH...SINGS"
Sappho, fragment 96

she spins across the floor carrying a cup of water
without spilling a drop

meanwhile,
astral fires & lifting their arms slowly like swans, they

run in zig-zags, careening   distance, weave
ellisional slides
orphic leaps
across sky/floor   tether / vault

Orion   dark matter

cast like wheat in a loom
starry feet, molten   flash

disappear in daylight   was/was not
                                                our feet

speed arc glint
                    overpass beat

Venus ⬤

waves and waves

shadows in grasses

⬤ *Arcturus*

thunder, river

hair loosened in time to

laminate

hive swarmed

music, undulant

our feet are blur, animal, air

⬤ *M14*

opalescent

PERFORMANCE NOTES:

Lyres, tuned to the Mixolydian mode Sappho invented, rhythmic drowse
of bees along dusty paths to Mithymna. Every sound crosses the senses
to evoke scent: green laureled grove

the smell of afternoons without a clock, of water without maps
a breathing world left unrecorded, unmeasured

Many dancers and singers, hundreds if necessary, draped with varying sizes
and types of sheepbells over soft clothing, the music and cadence

then made by their own bodies echoing the melodious chaos
of a flock of sheep returning to shelter at dusk, the theater dark as night

each body carries its own sound, like the cicada or lark, figures
as planets with flashing cymbals and swift feet

Clusters

of small

flashing

lights

affixed to

dancers'

bodies

spark like

fireflies or

constellations

in motion

1. six large offering cups made of white clay inscribed with the words: *reconciliation, human, enemy, trembling, wound, not-turning-away*

2. fragrant cedar branches <ΚΕΔΡΟΣ>

3. a list of damages sustained: x-rays, oral testimony, eyewitness reports

4. nest lit from above

5. fire: carried, extinguished and re-kindled

6. Eros — embodied in armfuls of red poppies

7. writing and recording devices: pencils, pens, palm pilots, γραφισ — for inscribing waxen tablets, to scrape into erasure, erosion tools, bees

THE HARROWING:

The theme is forgiveness, the theme is justice

(deferred, delayed, obtained). The theme is rejoicing

alternating with suffering *(watercourse, torrent)*

Harrowing the fields. Beauty (bound to a thing, entangled)

Making compassion possible

The lyre, lyric (our thirst — ζιφοσ). To frighten away

(chase, reject). A thicket of reeds (δονακευς)

Kindling a fire

What moves through the human body

Before and after the discovery of electricity

φ

As the lights, bells and dancers whirl, it's like hearing the inside
of silence   all the edges and interstices   the beautiful astringent

vertigo engendered by pure sound
a wild longing enters the hearer — imperceptibly, without resistance,

burnished   like oxygen in air, blue glazed, milky intemperate
close to the veins, veering toward

the impulse to weep without any reason — to cry out (ΓΟΟΣ) fiery
throated, sedimentary   the sounds we've never heard before   ashes,
resonance

to rock back and forth tenderly, to tremble like silvery olive leaves
to be filled with a crimson, carnelian   rose heat as a humming
grows around the heart

the sensation of vibrating wings (leaves, doves) acuity of sensate
burning,
a clarity — resinous, austere — that arises not so much by
understanding the sounds which fall away from us but by losing
the need

to comprehend   salts vanishing into chalk blue sea completely open
windowed

the mind which holds
our thoughts so tightly

now unfolds   into all the mineral brightness

of Sappho's night sky

to speak in smells, as one animal to another

I.

ravens calling at sunrise   how poplar stems smell, slightly
          & sunset   bitter where they join red and green
                                                    sun on granite
                    the heat inside
                                        what matters most

dirt close to the shovel, grease on axle bearings, red cloth smeared with
                    pine pollen and resin, fresh morning air:
                            a catch at the throat

     very cold and bright   locked aluminum casing, titanium

                    wire,   sparks across electrodes

     refrigerated egg,   an idea held
                                        tight and clear in the mind

Orion grows brighter,

smell of inches and leaves, the dust
                              of armchairs and books, copper

first sun in weeks   falling and falling inside yourself

          how wonderful: bright flicker of quartz

                    and numerous birds

     at the heart   filament and arc, seam of skin

                    the catch, the locket

the edge: net full of water

                         and equally empty

     what to give up and what to hold onto:

the interior of hair, the way he parts his hair to prove it's not a pelt, the
respectable man with his arms frantically upraised: "I am not an animal,"
he cries, all evidence to the contrary, "I am not an animal." Betrayed by
breath and bone, every pore, every follicle reveals, every smell, every
scrap of body betrays and saves us

               moving where?

     that paradise of upheaval,
                              the exact place
                         you find yourself
          now

III.

what you used to think was weak

smell of newly opened iris and lilacs

and now find is alive and incredibly strong

oak leaves under fresh snow

the story moving backward

sliding into thaw

excess of melting, joyous

ripe mulberries overhang

summer lake, floating

like a swan, a freefall

return to the world

read this book of rainwater

a book made entirely of smells and silence

reading the blank spaces

1.

a hawk circles the wild fig
violets bloom in the shade

it is a day no brighter than others

still, words bring their own light
and we turn our faces blindly toward them

2.

trying to read Sappho's honeycombed and eroded texts
is like listening to my mother tell of her life during the war —

everything left out is what we need to know

is it "*meteor*" or "*meter*"
"*respect*" or "*respite*"?

are we riding over or under the wave?

3.

scatter and fled, covered with road dust, lost in transit
ploughed by the shear forces of wind and exile

decipher this erased surface, the scarred geologic
strata of memory

stories without a beginning, middle or end:

— unknown face half devoured by shadow
— patterns of a carpet or carved armoire
— forgetting the word for mulberry: *szeder*
— fruit that stains your hands black
— the scent of wool after rain
— fresh milk
— across the horizon something like αστραπε, lightning flashes

let the night fall in on itself

4.

all I could learn about the war and her exile
came from the pressure of frozen foods shaping silence

the acute, negative space outlined by TV dinners with their
aluminum compartments and satellite patterned melmac

dinnerware leaning into the unspoken

5.

cartography of exile

where we pursue   not the deer, but the trail
of her absence   [which tells us more]   tracking

not the object of desire, but the entire field —

fierce and unmarked wilderness that sustains her

the sun's other face

"*Like bees, their metabolism stimulated at a certain temperature, we swarm to the indeterminate: attempt to enter the very vocables that history, inadvertently or not, has left open.*"
— Gustav Sobin

My hand reaches into the cool space left open in a chapel of dimly lit
saints, safe in green shuttered sanctuary. Outside — sudden brightness

eclipses the mind — nothing remains solid in the light where Sappho
wrote *"love has obtained for me the brightness and beauty of the sun,"*

this light effaces form, swarms fields like powder the mind sees dark
as readily, heavy pitted rock disappears into shimmer, into its

own mica rendered transparent lithic, rent open into honeycombed
cicada heat coming upon an oleander grove

with its turtles and underground springs — πελε: the same word for
[streams of milk] and [source of fire] as with thunder and fruit, as with

the hidden interior and the shine the world wears over itself like rare
cloth, like black netting tangled in olive branches harvesting what

the sun's body throws away, this overflow of thick glare, glass, opaque,
seeing obliterates what is visible in order to see more clearly, in order

to find the intimate absence here, always next to us breathing, to turn
light dark as the erased hollow of a wave which makes it a wave

whose furled shape is rendered blind in our ears as concaved sound,
in this moment, a cicada lands on my dress: clear wings, heavy body,

and it is understood now, the sun has made us understand how clarity
is evidence of its opposite, shadowed truth translated in carved air

as longing enters black & red clay

"*mixed with all kinds of colors*"
— Sappho, fragment 152

crushed pigment in layers — devotional   iron oxide, yellow cactus spine
rockface cliffs "thinking in paint" always close to the edge
ochre & lime plummet sedimentary within a hairsbreadth glint of archaic

in painting, we are told, there are "no clean hands"
stained with the suddenness of what is hidden
scratch the ground with a stick: find a mirror there

rattle made with small stones, corn husk & green corn on the kitchen table,
Sappho's heaps of gravel: χεραδοσ, telegraphic fragments clear as

the underside of a crow's wing, the color of sky and wind

uneven surface
of a pearl   here you can smell copal incense, piñon pitch, chamiso
blooming invisible flowers, to sail out with a cobalt prow
traveling toward the extreme interior — heart pounding

composite dissimilars

necessary for binding, this overlay

until heat   the way grasses are born, earth's volatile resins, starry
spills over us   ultramarine, ores   seeds falling in clouds, pale cornmeal

rust red chilpotle, saffron dyed robe — earth makes

colors so we can fall in love with dirt

try composing a pile of ashes, anything that spins or cracks
wandering stars <πλανετεσ> the color of golden fruit
nesting resilient

this is how to work with what is given — small incidents moving

breath by breath

the scintillant underlayer, ocean resident in rock

deerbone dragged
over shale

        calcium magnet, distillate, scalded

        a single rose   pale as fur
isolate, combed

there's a woman speaking on the telephone, somewhere inside her voice
a secret resides

        eggs, milky
        sap, water
locked familiar, inviolate
and fragile as the brain in its skull

        ears washed over
        with the sound of willow
a tiny flame   leaves
in each living cell

       dear S: I am trying to trace your words here in this lava flow of signs
where the earth is written with birds doubled at the heart over wheeling
stars and the sign ΣΠΕΙΡΑ: slow curve of a snake unwinding as we pray

to attain that sleek mind

        red earth, green water: the writing we cannot translate
        surrounds us

       as though what the human hand touches here
    still remains wild
            ash and smoke, a little cloud of breath
        crushed juniper, mica in tire track treads

      clear white washed over blue green agave, our bright
obsidian selves flicker like radio waves

     carbon turned to skin,
        quickened   torrent of vowels

pigmented, pressed into clay   into a world open and porous as rain,
       into plants streaming with fevers unknown to us, into countless

bodies, microbes, silica, into shell edge and dust, chromatic throat

      a voice like your own

musa de "flor y fruto"
muse of "flower and fruit"

The resemblance to Frida Kahlo increases —
sitting still, slightly amused, archaic, vast

wearing intricate skirts next to deep azul
courtyard walls and a profusion of morning glory
tangled with jasmine — aromatic, languorous

face that shimmers : self painted ikon

to bring the sun down, illuminate
like a scar

"materia su mis ojos" she writes:

matter in my eyes

"tenderness can also be this blue"

"blue: the sea, the sky, the unknown"

a stone to pound open green
almond husks — white inside

the seed inside the seed

finding the moon reflected in waves

∴

another mystery: the deep blue
sea made of clear water

how our eyes create love

lumen: light, eye, opening

"and the whole place shadowed by roses"
                    — Sappho, fragment 2

shadow cast by the moving shade
of plane trees

voluntary blindness, acquired patiently
with great & hopeless effort

                    a place so deep
light can only enter as an
idea   plummeting more deeply into

this unclothed   abundance
            "empty space or

missing part":   *hollowed : lumened*

luein   < λυειν >   a loosening

lyre of · · · · · · · · *unbound light*

threshing the word

SAPPHO AND A PARTICLE PHYSICS OF LANGUAGE

The visible world is made of three particles: the electron, the "up quark" and the "down quark," which are "actually those uncuttable 'atoms' first imagined 2500 years ago by the Greeks — pointlike, indivisible particles from which the world around us blossoms."

— Gordan Kane, *The Particle Garden*

threshing the word

What if we could look at language as matter — *[as real and outside our imagining as granite or cedar trees]* and move inside words, the way particle physicists break into atoms with the force of their own energy and light?

To track the intelligent chaos of language by threshing open the word,

                              olive pressed against stone
                              disappears into
its own
wet interior   vowels in their syllables
                              wheat crushed white

as the almond in its green husk.

Delving into the fibers and roots of the word *fragment* [Sappho's emblem, her surviving] first unbinds the alliterative echo of "*fragrant*"

                   [redolent of sunflower pollen,
basil on a white plate, a single dark
crimson rose]

floating free from the solid core of definition, from meaning one thing alone as a river of other words is loosened, like sodium and chloride molecules from the simple compound salt.

And we discover *fragment* arises from the Latin *frangere* which comes from *bhreg:* to break or breach — in French: *brier* or *broyer:* to knead

[as in *brioche* — yeasty and warm in the morning as violets bloom]

related to *brak-* :
undergrowth, bracken: "that which impedes motion":

[ferny thickets, refuge of mallows and plover eggs,
shelter for the undomesticated: outcasts and resistance fighters]

While *break* continues to fragment like a splintered, living shard
and no longer green, vine-tangled growth, *brak-* becomes *braeke:*

"a crushing instrument":   its own winnowing ring

threshing open a chorus of words fragmented from all hope
of referring singly and without complication

to the myriad tesserae of their sources:

FRACAS,   FRACTED,   FRACTION,
FRACTURE, FRAGILE, FRANGIBLE,
FRAIL,   INFRACT,   INFRINGE,
OSSIFRAGE   <the osprey hawk or bone
breaking bird>, REFRACT, SAXIFRAGE
<"rock breaking herb: small flowered with
rosette leaves"> and on to SUFFRAGARI (to
vote for: "to use a broken piece of tile as
a ballot">: SUFFRAGIUM: the right to vote.

It is not impossible to imagine Sappho grown pale and fierce at a hunger
strike in a circle of other women who will not be swayed. And as she speaks,

we can barely distinguish just under her voice, low and indistinct

the sound of threshing and threshing — the fragments of *fragment*
like a waterwheel of cicadas at dusk.

It's not hard to locate Sappho at this overlay of electrons swarming the throat

each fragment refusing the reduction by which it is defined —

opening instead into a welter of infinity

Sappho's fragments [*"first imagined 2500 years ago"*]
threshed by the "crushing instruments" of time and censors:

broken open but not broken
her own shards scatter like pollen into our lives

"— pointlike, indivisible particles from which the world around us blossoms."

This is how she keeps writing her way back to us
with an aching persistence

like the almost invisibly flowered saxifrage chiseling into rock

and the white-winged velocity of the osprey.

lexicon of the muse

Aphrodite's

Large plane trees, leaves rattling in the wind. Also:
silver on the underside of olives, honeycombed bees.
Bells at dusk, mirrors. Violet light around the moon.
Anything shaped Δ or $\vee$. And waves: salt water's engine.

Bells

echo all morning. First doves, then cicadas, then doves again.
In the courtyard tangled with cobalt morning glories, a country
and western song on the radio keeps time with the sound of women
sweeping stone paths with water.

The sacred makes noise everywhere it can.

Cowry shells

Sewn with bells on the leather neckbands
of sheep. Evidence of ancient trade routes,
why she is sometimes called Black Athena.

Dolphins

Sighted earlier that day, beyond the harbor. A young Artemis girl
fights in play with the men at the taverna. If she weren't smiling,
she would scare them to death.

Eftalou

Hot springs, shallow tide pools, translucent seaweed.
White domed building: openings scattered across the ceiling
like stars for light and swallows to enter and cross overhead.

The body feels like a small boat floating.

Fig trees

The fruit stays green a long time
turning itself into sun.

Garden

From Apostolo's house on the edge of town, you look straight across dry
fields and the Aegean to Asia Minor. He was 18 years at sea — the garden
blooms from seeds collected from all over the world. There are beehives,
almond trees, dahlias, daylilies and the round, small leaved basilico.
After coffee, Apostolo brings out the shards he finds at work
digging up the streets.

Here, in an empty peanut can: a buckle, two clay pipes. And the head
of Sappho, the size of his thumb.

Hammered

metal plaques: offerings hung by the altar in shaded light: a lady, child,
gentleman, a foot, leg, eyes — as though everything that can be named
carries its own prayer.

Intense

heat at midday stops work. We enter some other dream,
the world of night by our side in wide open sunlight.

Kalloni

All along the fertile plain of Kalloni, oleanders, pine and olive groves flash
across bus window shiny with beads, saints and blue glass against
the evil eye. We are driving into the heart of flowering —
a countryside of bees.

Karaghiosis

Early evening, in an open air courtyard, the shadow puppet theater begins.
Human sized stick figures are lit up from behind translucent curtains.
The puppets are painted in black outlining bright primary colors,
like stained glass windows or butterfly wings. They move like Punch
& Judy, jumping and beating each other with sticks, speaking in gravelly
Greek voices, tracing ancient routes out of Indonesia and India.

Persistence of guerrilla theater, occupation and resistance (on the walls
current graffiti denounces the u.s. and NATO). There's an enormous, opulent
Turkish residence on one side and the small Greek domos on the other.
The wily, long-nosed Greek puppet, like Coyote, outsmarts his opponent
all evening.

Behind us, a grandmother lets her empty carriage roll down the walkway.
A child wanders down and opens the stage door, revealing
the puppeteers at work. The moon grows brighter overhead.

LITERATURE

Abalone shell — eroded as the cliffs: coral exterior,
smooth pearlescent layers, thin as paper. Water's motion
written deeply into its form: perfect, unreadable sentences.

LUNA

At moonrise Strato says a poem for the moon that the women taught him.
He shows us how to herd sheep by throwing a rock in the air and yelling
o o o t — o o o t — b r r r. The full moon is clear over the rocky hillsides.
Strato holds out a branch of green almonds the size of eggs.

MIDDAY

We find her walking toward us — eyes half closed — in the center
of the narrow stone street.

MITHYMNA

Passing old women in black at dusk: *kalespera, kalespera —*
the sound of the evening star *hesperus* in their voices.

MUSICA

In fields by the cemetery, I've been recording the sound
of sheep and their bells as they run in many different timbres

and rhythms. When I hand the earphones over to the shepherd,
his face transforms listening to his own flock as though they called
to him from another world. *Musica,* we say, *oraira:* beautiful.
Sitting close enough to the sheep until they forget me,
their music becomes thistles and wind at dusk.

NAI:

the sound *yes* makes in the sweep of the broom, Euterpe's low
throaty humming as she clears her courtyard, the sound of thistles,
and doves, the turning over of a small car's engine, sails flapping loose
in the wind. Even refusal makes a place for us, a break in the surface
of ideas.

NIGHT

The sky and ocean meet and exchange places in the dark —
are we walking in the starry firmament or shifting water?
Even dreams are more solid.

ODYSSEUS

works with very small puppets for a theater group in Paris near les Halles
and returns home every summer. We stand in front of what was the mayor's
old villa, shaded in plane trees, entirely overrun with roses:
"all the intelligentsia were there."

Also: the postman, riding his moped through the narrow stone walkways,
exactly two donkeys wide, with baskets on either side.

Intelligence of vines and olive groves, conversations without the pressure of arrival, letters carried and never sent. Returning home an entire lifetime.

ψ

A lame fisherman cleans his catch. At night, lights hung from the small boats echo the stars.

⊙

At the edge of town, the temple of Apollo — across from an old woman's house, near the bare shade of her apricot tree.

Sanctuary in the eyes and in the palm of the hand.

∴

Old stone house, given over to bats and mice. Elegant row of cypress: the air heavy with bees and sleep. Abandoned well under fig trees near grapes and oleander. Dry grasses, green pomegranates. Roses too dry to flower. Black netting hung in olive tree branches, the silver on their leaves like thoughts.

On this island, Sappho named what we see: water, olive tree, doves — so that there is no separating the fruit and what shines from it.

The body is a woman, her spirit is a body, is a rose, is beloved, like the olive.

Πετρα

Off the bus, near the Women's Agricultural Cooperative
in Petra. Along paths up the mountainside to Petri: a lizard,
green turtle and snake head. Poplars, figs, mostly olives — the skin
and quills of a porcupine. There are fresh springs in channels running
along walkways in the village, across the courtyard into the church.

Quiet

Rough sand in the cove: thin-ribbed shells, deep blue
mussels, a sienna colored starfish pressed flat and secret:
what we can find looking inside ourselves.

Roses

struggle for water in front of the library's glaring white marble stairs.
Next to windows overlooking the sea, two women crochet in the cool
rooms, keepers of this cave of written knowledge.

Shepherds

There's Costa, with a scarf on his head, his two dogs: Daisy and Micro.
In an old photograph he's wearing wide-legged Turkish style pants,
immense moustaches and carries a rifle. He pours endless, thick
Turkish coffee and brags about his herd: fifty πρoβατα.

At an afternoon party to celebrate the cassette player he has just traded
for a sheepskin, Costa sets a table under fig trees and serves cakes, plates

of melon, metaxa and more Turkish coffee. The recorder plays
his music energetically from its place of honor in the center of the table.
Two respectable ladies are invited, one speaks French, the other English,
also a college age nephew, Odysseus, a little girl. And there's a shy older
shepherd, who stays on the edge of our group. All at once, he climbs
like a swift wild animal up the tree to see if the figs are ripe yet
(knowing they aren't).

Squid

dries like laundry — twisted nylon hosiery — on the trellis
of the Paradise Taverna at Naxos.

Taverna

Tzaziki, potatoes, delicate cod in butter, koreotiki, souvlakia, ouzo,
white Lesbos wine, melons.

Traffic

Temples rise above Athens' traffic as if they too were speeding across
time — in absolute stillness.

White marble, congestion, smog, cool green trellised walkways
and shuttered rooms.

Karpousi: small, very sweet watermelons.

Thistles growing at the edge of the runway.

Undergrowth

Turtles live near the springs among oleanders. Nearby, up the hillside:

a chapel the size of a shed. Tall thistles on the path, swallow's nest
at the door and a wasp hive: all variations of shrines.

Villa

decaying elegantly like thick opera records with worn grooves.
Rusty iron gates, the sound of singing in French from the shuttered window.
A fig shaped woman carrying laundry blocks the entryway.

Entrance across the threshold is a kind of entrancement,
even into an ordinary room.

Widow

After two Greek husbands, now she wants an English one.

Winnowing ring

The first theater: a circle of stones. I think of my grandfather, strapped
to the threshing mill like a mule, covered white with raw, crushed flour.

White line

The morning smells of wet barley, trampled mud and sedge.
Herons continue to design the marshes — standing or flying,
moving or still.

How are words separate from their white wings?
How is their motion like an idea inside us?

Words

The old woman at the sweater store reads English books cut into
thirds so they are easier to carry on the bus. Reading, she says,
is better than speaking — the way people talk is too irregular,
too hard to understand. In books, the words are perfect.

X

The taxi driver crosses himself before setting out into city traffic at dawn.

The letter which is a motion we make for what we can't say.

Mystery within mysteries:

groves of olives & palms, traffic jams, a drop of water in a leaf's
ridge, choros, harmonics, light spilling out of nowhere

light spilling out of the heart of γ and ζ.

site of luminous concussion

MY FIRST MUSE

"with gold laurel they bind their hair"
— Edith Hamilton, *Mythology*

my unconscious brought me back
Wide Memory — body vast as the Milky Way
mother of all *violet-wreathed* Muses

her wellspring lined with pale cypress, water too cold for the mind to drink
so we forget as we remember, throat aflame

I'M SIXTEEN AND STARE AT CAMUS' FACE

as though it were an ikon, capable of speaking
reliquary of compressed sun, concentrated reflective surface

mineral   //   bees   //   magnetite

large wave before it breaks

UNDER DRIFTS OF WHITE FLOWERING

apple trees, new grasses, wings in air
all the living world finds refuge inside the tiny photograph
where he lives. Immanence can be sensed, ironic —

against the sun-glared wall
dark hair, furrowed brow

[   ]   eyes half closed,
looking down and inward
with a dizzying velocity that stuns gravity
[   ]

BODY TURNED AT THE SLIGHT ANGLE OF AN ANTI/HERO

Ορφευς with a cigarette in the corner of his mouth
Αχίγευς in blue jeans, *Πενθευς* standing at the corner, brooding

making estrangement a shrine

ΑΛΣ: salt
ΑΛΣ: the sea
ΑΛΣΟΣ: place grown with trees and grasses

= sacred grove   bitterness overcome by its own heat

"why is thy shine greater at night?"
"why is every star extinguished in fire?"
"what is blue and what do we think of blue?"

enters, hovers, gazes

the story has been told before

how he dies in storm-gray waves cresting tall
as a mountain, in a meteor shower

bright and swift as lava, in a collision

against a plane tree outside Villeblevin
papers scattered on the road in the night

tire tracks, broken glass

"they drew you across steep air down to the black earth"
— Sappho, fragment 1

I CANNOT IMAGINE ANYONE MORE

present

SO WHERE AM I REACHING TOWARD?

empty mirror, death, future beloved?

MUSE

EMBEDDED IN LANGUAGE: TWIG FROM OLIVE TREE
SMALL FIG <   > ASHES

Camus means *snub-nosed*

and the verb *muse* takes its roots from
museau, muzzle, snout: *"to cast about for a scent"*

he could have been called Albert Museau or Albert Muse

(nxnɛis):   sounding, roaring, echoing
(étincelles):   sparks from voice-breath

light burning in on itself

C(amus): *"WE ARE WALKING TO MEET LOVE AND DESIRE"*

salt, resin, quartz, milk

S(appho): *"SOMETIMES SHE CLOSED HER EYES / ALL NIGHT LONG"*

pulse beating faintly at the wrist, petals

C: *"IN THIS GREAT CONFUSION OF WIND AND SUN*
WHICH MIXES RUINS WITH LIGHT"

white noise

S: "tenderer than the rose"

C: "a pomegranate tree unfurled its flowers"

she has turned toward the shadow which makes her face even clearer

S: "Brightness and [
   [   ]

— strange joy   (C)
— the dress   (S)
— handbag   (S)

entirely without shame:
washed

somnolence   chaleur
                    colonnes luisantes

    shining   columns

              heat   cyprès

entering the landscape of the muse in Camus' pages

the sound of cicadas rose in my Oakland room though it would be
years until I would hear *[les cigales]* *[ηχετης]* outside of literature

ανισον

"crushing absinthe between my fingers"   — Camus
"purple, perfumed"   — Sappho, fragment 101

wild anise on the hillsides, sage where blue-bellied lizards
scatter among live oak, manzanita sheltering deer

Camus' North African coast awakens here

in ridges and dry creek beds right off the MacArthur Freeway's
drone, the sound of cicadas dazes the mind

and *the sun turns black*

his collected essays, Gallimard, about two thousand pages with red ribbons
to mark passages, leather binding the color of crushed berries, paper thin
as cigarette wrappers but tough almost translucent, unusually
light and easy to hold — about the size of my hand

διαδερκομει: to see
τραμμενος: turned toward the sun
πελεια: a dove
υαλοs: transparent stone

    burning glass : concave lens

NOT TO DISTURB BY READING COVER TO COVER

like a newspaper — as though you were to get information
from it rather than initiation

IN THE SPRING

we are torn apart by flowering
raw blue sky, opaque sea

mangled : chalky

e]nter in this kingdom of ru[ins
] we are spectators [
] end of a few steps, the [
] throat. Their essence ferments [
] sun rises over all the [
gen?]erous that makes [   ] vacillate
meet]ing of love and of [
] lessons, neither the bitter phil[osphy
gran]deur. Outside the sun [
w]ild everything appears to us [
] to be alone there. I am [   ] there [
] I love [and I read from [
] sea which absorbs me entirely [
r]uins of spring [
] loses [
i]n nature [
] nature has given everything away [
] red toward [
] temples and places [
] much science [
] has brought [
to]day finally their [
] how many hours [
] the ruins [
] wild [
] eyes and [
] filled with [

Camus fragment: Noces

ORCHARDS OF EMPTY SPACE

spread around vast by wind
what is stolen   :   gone wider

site of luminous concussion

TREMBLING AT THE EDGE

sparrow, swallow   crescent flight
fall   unwinged

all the names for human love made visible:

beautiful-shining
beautiful-sounding
with-beautifully-flowing-eddies
with-beautiful-colts
with-beautiful-leaves
beautiful-voiced

oblivion witness

volumes and volumes of open pages
resembling the vast unwritten

shine of light on water

1. Matter
2. lower air ($\alpha\epsilon\rho$) — atmosphere we breathe
3. Nietzsche
4. the word that means long-haired, feathered arrow,
   leafy, grassy — a comet

"the world always ends up overcoming history"
"le monde toujours finit par vaincre l'histoire"

CAMUS INTERVIEW, 1959

When asked about the cinema, turns the question adroitly
back to the questioner. When asked to describe himself

"the most significant trait of your character," answers

"that depends on the day. But often, a heavy and blind stubbornness."
[Thick as mud] [Impenetrable — another deflection]

As for a definition of the indefinable: "You have once written

'secret of my universe: imagine God without the immortality of the soul.'
Can you make this thought more precise?"

*"Yes. I have a sense of the sacred and I don't believe in a future life.
That's all."*

— What are your six most favorite words?
— *Allumer, absurde, zéro, désert, lucidité, impossible*
  And also: monde — to which all the above apply.
  World illuminated, absurd, zero, desert, lucid, impossible

— What do you think of death?
— *Et vous?*

— Where is blue appropriate?
— *Blue streets, crowds, heart, blue storage, Communists, 1956, blue*
  razor, silence

EXILE

The muse has vanished, fled, skedaddled, gone
bolted, dissolved, dispersed, evaporated, walked out the door

been disappeared, obscured, written over, lost

the pattern of wind over water
the pattern of yes and no

many little waves cresting
and slipping under

MOVED TO A COUNTRY MADE OF SMOKE, MY MOTHER'S WORLD

hovering around the rooms I entered returning from high school

the atmosphere thick with smoke (ΚΑΠΝΟΣ), the sound of records
playing Piaf's laments and Camus reading from *L'Étranger*
in his Pied Noir accent

everything oblique, slant, indistinct, equivocal

σκιαγραφos (skia-graphos): shadow-writing
painted in light and shadow — a refugee's refuge from English

like Ovid's Eurydice *"fugit fumare"* — who fled into smoke

WHY THERE ARE NINE MUSES INSTEAD OF ONE

polyphonic : music from many

can be lost and found at the same time

"DANS LE BLEU DE TOUTE L'IMMENSITÉ"
— Piaf, *L'Hymne à l'amour*

in this blue immensity
the records echo (εχο) a country she could reinhabit

not Hungary ever again as home

her New World found somewhere
in smoke and sound — displaced

splintered light

tunneling through language

IN HUNGARIAN, MUSE IS *MUZSA*

when she speaks, doves rustle
in poplars

the coffee grows darker
and more complex

tram cars
glisten on their rails

oh — there's a river, a river
shining

and the birds listen
when we call to them

*és mi mindent megétünk, amit
a madarak nekünt mondanak*

and we understand everything the birds say to us

bird   :   shining   :   river
¥   Ω   Δ

YOUR WAY HOME   GRAIN BACK TO WHEAT

across what can't be crossed

WHEN IS A HOMELAND?   IN WHAT COUNTRY

can you go home, that place where they
speak your own language, the one you've forgotten

singing it so hard into body's silence

BROKEN LINE OVER MOUNTAINS, FLEEING

in the dark gorge leading the horses on foot
"earth with its wide roads gaped"
         — Homeric hymn to Demeter as Persephone is seized

Höllental, 1945 Austrian Alps

THERE IS NO GOING BACK

even if maps show you all the roads and paths
and bridges in the world

obstinate   —   *heavy and blind*

broken open like an empty cup

SO THE MOON LOOSENS ITS LIGHT IN ANOTHER COUNTRY

and petals fall there also and salt is blessed
at the table   the fragrance from open windows

is similar and not the same, erased

by presence

grove

TWO SMALL ESSAYS

two small essays

fragments

Sappho is carried to us through history in fragments and stays alive
in fragments when her own work must have always appeared to her as
whole, fused entirely with voice and music, never shattered or
marginalized:

> THERE WAS NEITHER . . . NOR SHRINE . . .
> FROM WHICH WE WERE ABSENT. NO GROVE
> . . . NOR DANCE . . . SOUND.   — fragment 94

And the fragments through which she reaches us are not simple fractures.
They carry an interior dissolving, the echo and emptiness at the inside
of a sentence, words eaten away in their veins like honeycombed gall and
worm rot, pulmonary collapse. Instead of the slow, comforting erosion of
nature and time, rock rubbed smooth by wind, Sappho's words are revised
by erasure, flame of the book burners and accident.

Which is why any survival of her voice

is evidence of random miracles, necessary to the uncensored chaos
which pours into the DNA of our shared intelligence and heart.

I am convinced that it is not so much a matter
of her survival in these fragments which is at stake

but our own.

muse : silence

Perhaps the roots and impulses of lyric poetry are tangled here in
Sappho's tesserae — a moving collage of inscape, tresses, epiphany,
moonlight, roses, eros.

Just to see what we're up against, consider what Robert Graves wrote:

> A woman who concerns herself with poetry should, I believe,
> either be a silent Muse and inspire the poets with her womanly
> presence . . . or she should be the Muse in a complete sense . . .
> and should write in each of these capacities with antique authority.
> She should be the visible moon: impartial, loving, severe, wise.

Could we say that Graves has mistaken his Muse as a noun (whose mystery
he persists in attempting to control), as a gender (ditto) — have we ever
made the same mistake?

Coming face to face with the Muse in this post-millennial flood of an
unleashed free market, for the first time I can begin to believe in the
domino theory, seeing it unfold in reverse — what checks and balances
do we have for unfettered buying and selling?

Perhaps the Muse (or rather whatever embodies our capacity to muse)
can stand alongside our Cold War ghosts in simple counterbalance
to the vast and inexorable engines of the free market

can stand for whatever in our lives and the world cannot be sold, bought,
made profitable, traded, translated into currency or debt

thin sapling against the rain, cliff face,
wing in the wind — agents of illumination
and resistance.

Most of the quotations of Sappho in this book are from *Greek Lyric,* vol. 1, *Sappho and Alcaeus,* edited and translated by David Campbell (Cambridge: Harvard University Press, 1982–1993). Quotations on pages 11, 50, and 52 are from *Archilochos, Sappho, Alkman: Three Lyric Poets of the Late Greek Bronze Age,* translated, with an introduction, by Guy Davenport (Berkeley: University of California Press, 1980).

Greek to English definitions have been gathered from *A Lexicon: Abridged from Liddell and Scott's Greek-English Lexicon* (1949; reprint, Oxford: Oxford University Press, 1966). Etymological references are derived from *The American Heritage Dictionary of the English Language,* edited by William Morris (Boston: Houghton Mifflin, 1981).

Camus is quoted from "Le Vent à Djémila," "Noces à Tipasa," and the 1959 interview "Réponses à Jean-Claude Brisville" in *Essais* (Paris: Gallimard, 1965). Translations from the French are by the author.

SAPPHO'S SPARROWS

inhabited by your absence
"only one complete poem . . .": See David Campbell's introduction to *Sappho and Alcaeus,* xii.

pleiades choreographic
"One Greek word . . .": Louise Bogan, "The Pleasures of Formal Poetry," *The Poet's Work,* edited by Reginald Gibbons (Boston: Houghton Mifflin, 1979), 208.

the sun's other face
Gustav Sobin: *Luminous Debris* (Berkeley: University of California Press, 1999), 157.

as longing enters red & black clay
"thinking in painting" and "no clean hands": See James Elkins, *What Painting Is* (New York: Routledge, 1999), 3, 5.

musa de "flor y fruto"
Frida Kahlo: See *The Diary of Frida Kahlo: An Intimate Self-Portrait,* edited by Phyllis Freeman, translated by Barbara de Toledo and Ricardo Pohlenz (New York: Harry Abrams Publishers, 1995), 211, 239.

THRESHING THE WORD

"her own shards scatter like pollen . . .": In 1905 Einstein interpreted the Brownian motion of pollen grains in water to prove the existence of atoms: "water molecules, being always in motion, were bombarding the pollen from all sides, causing its motion. . . . Finally, after 2500 years, the existence of atoms was universally accepted." Gordan Kane, *The Particle Garden: Our Universe as Understood by Particle Physicists* (Reading, Mass.: Addison-Wesley, 1995), 30.

SITE OF LUMINOUS CONCUSSION

MY FIRST MUSE
"with gold laurel . . .": Edith Hamilton, *Mythology* (1940; reprint, New York: New American Library, 1969), 68.

MELPOMENE
Villeblevin: Site of collision on the road to Paris where Camus died in 1960.

ENOUGH TO READ AS A CHANT
Camus fragments are taken from "Noces à Tipasa" torn into strips, like the papyrus texts used as wrappings from which most of Sappho's fragments have been gathered.

"DANS LE BLEU DE TOUTE L'IMMENSITÉ"
"L'Hymne à l'amour": Sung by Piaf, written by Marguerite Monnot.

"IN HUNGARIAN, MUSE IS *MUZSA*"
Keeping close to the original (Doric) Greek *Moisa*.

BROKEN LINE OVER MOUNTAINS, FLEEING
"earth with its wide roads . . .": *Homeric Hymns,* translated by Apostolos Athanassakis (Baltimore: Johns Hopkins University Press, 1976), 2.

Höllental, 1945: When I found this photograph in an Upper Michigan antique store, it reminded me of Persephone's descent into Hades as pictured in childhood mythology books. Later, when my mother translated diaries she kept as she was fleeing Hungary with her family at the end of World War II, I read that they came through this same Höllental pass in the Austrian Alps at night with horse and wagon led on foot over the steep terrain.

GROVE

muse : silence
Robert Graves: Quoted from *The White Goddess* (New York: Farrar, Strauss and Giroux, 1972), 447.